Praise for **Welcome Home**

"*Holly Hudspeth will take you through the most exquisite tour of your emotional home! Her clever and insightful metaphors will give you lifelong visuals to empower yourself as you walk together through each room of your house. She may not know you personally, but you will have a personal encounter that will shift your perspective and your life if you allow it. She will remind you that you can chose boldness over brokenness, faith over fear and power over pain.* **Welcome Home** *is a companion guide for anyone who has been overrun by anxiety and needs the voice of someone who has cracked the code on how to overcome the battle. The book is insightful, well-researched and filled with practical tools you can use right away. Knowing Holly personally, I hear her voice in the penned words and that will be a gift to you.*"

> – **May Bagnell**, Author, Women's Lifestyle Coach & Photographer and Care Coach at Bagnell Brain Center in Miami, FL.

"*This book is so powerful, and it will deeply impact all who read it! Thank you for being courageous and disciplined enough to pour your soul and insight into these pages.*

This is more than a book – it is a companion that will guide you to soul level freedom and lasting peace. These pages will give you courage to face the heaviest aspects of your human experience, bring you into deep awareness of the power of your own being and equip you with practical tools to holistically calm anxiety and maximize your capacity."

> – **Jessica Willis**, MA, BCCC, Solace Counselling

"WOW!! Anyone who is or who has ever experienced the debilitating effects of anxiety must read this book. Holly Hudspeth is a genius. The way she has used her creativity to spread her message and her own experience to help and to heal is alluring. This book is more than another self-help book to add to your bookshelf, this is a work of art that you will take with you and know that you are understood and that you can get through your own unique experience with anxiety. You will feel like Holly is there with you, holding your hand, as you move through your own experience. She is whispering "It is ok, you are ok. Listen to the whisper of your heart, it knows the way." Thank you Holly for bringing such a gift to the world. Your beautifully written book is about to help so many."

   – **Suzana Mihajlovic**, CEO Your 2 Minds,
     Elite Performance and Mindset Coach, Author.

Welcome HOME

EVICTING THE GHOST OF ANXIETY

HOLLY HUDSPETH

Published by
Hasmark Publishing
www.hasmarkpublishing.com

Permission should be addressed in writing to Holly Hudspeth at www.HealWithHolly.com

Editor: Corinne L. Casazza
corinnecasazza@gmail.com

Cover & Book Design: Anne Karklins
anne@hasmarkpublishing.com

ISBN 13: 978-1-989756-04-1
ISBN 10: 1989756042

*I dedicate this book to all of the wonderful people
who struggle each day with anxiety.
May this book aid you in your road to victory.*

Share your wins at www.HealWithHolly.com

Medical Disclaimer
This content is not intended to be a substitute for professional medical
advice, diagnosis, or treatment. Always seek the advice of your physician
or other qualified health provider with any questions you have regarding
a medical condition.

Acknowledgments

I want to thank all the people who stressed me out. They have added more material for this book than I can ever thank them for. They have tirelessly stepped on my dreams and every time I was ready to succeed, they were there to discourage me. Their impact on my life is more than I can actually express. They made me hate my life and caused me to move on. They have provided the moral support of a soggy noodle and they were more than happy to help me become mediocre. I want to extend special thanks to everyone that thinks that I am talking about them, because in a small insignificant way I am.

However, there are a few people to whom I do owe gratitude. My son, Haven for being the best Robin that any Batman could ask for. My friend Dorothy Mullet who truly supported me in the tough times of life; and Eileen Mullet for injecting this project with all her enthusiasm. To my friends Pam Satterfield and Tara Bradshaw; love you guys. And to all the myriad of unnamed supporters, thank you.

– Holly Hudspeth

Table of Contents

Introduction

*"Too many of us are not living our dreams
because we are living our fears."*

~ Les Brown

In America today, chronic stress, anxiety and panic are constant companions for most of the population. It is the thing we all talk around, but few really admit how much this issue is robbing them of their hopes, dreams and peace on a daily basis. There are the few who wear their anxiety like a badge of honor. They cause the rest of us to hide any admission of nervousness out of fear of being categorized as being one of 'those people.'

While countless articles discuss the anxiety problem over 17 million Americans are facing daily, it hasn't always been that way. When I was a child, I was isolated in my sensitivity to stress. In college, I don't recall anyone but my best friend ever having a problem with anxiety that they talked about. I knew better than to openly admit my penchant for panic, although I did have people refer to me as "a nervous little creature" upon occasion. When it came to fight or flight, I had a heavy flight response. I could run so fast for apparently no reason it seemed as though I simply disappeared. As I matured, my fight or flight response began to include "freeze!" That stress response replaced my previous flight and created a feeling of being stuck in my life.

Having a good sense of humor about myself kept me from completely going off the deep end. The truth is that it was really hard to be me. I searched for years to "fix" my nervous system so I could enjoy life on any given day. It took a lifetime, but I accomplished that, and I intend to help you get started on your own journey of self-discovery to identify and correct the root cause of your chronic stress and anxiety issues once and for all.

Perhaps like me, you were a sensitive child. I sensed things that others did not. I also noticed the details of people's auras. If someone was angry or impatient it would crush my inner being, whether they were feeling that way toward me or not. Their energy seemed to fill the room and I was acting as a lightning rod to absorb that negative energy. Being young and unable to express what was happening to me, I had no one to tutor me in how to navigate my way through a crowd of people or observe without absorbing. I grew up feeling like my sensitivity was a weakness rather than a gift; at times in my young life it caused me to hate myself for being so weird.

Because I didn't know what energy was mine and what was the vibe, mood or energetic field of those around me, my level of trust in myself from a young age was very low and I had a lot of confusion. This insecurity caused me to pick up on subtle nuances like a hawk, and yet somehow miss the obvious when it came to knowing who to trust.

The first panic attack I ever had happened when I was 16 during an event that was supposed to be fun. The conditions that supported this sudden shift in my reality were invited by my own teenage stupidity. Basically, it was my own fault because I didn't think before I got in the car with some people I really didn't need to be hanging out with. I had no idea reality could fold in on itself so quickly. It never crossed my mind that the people I was hanging out with weren't good people. My blueprint of how that outing would go did not at all match what happened. I blamed myself for being with the wrong people. But, how could I know something about someone that they were intentionally hiding from me? If it was my fault I could have prevented it, but I didn't do anything wrong. I was just riding in the car.

My intuition that had always been so sharp, failed me that night, eroding my trust at a point in my life that was critical for my sense of security and belonging in this world. Having an intuitive gift AND an anxiety issue made it sometimes impossible to distinguish a warning in my spirit from an overreaction in my nervous system. It left me feeling as if something bad was always about to happen.

From that point forward, the looming possibility that people and events may not be as they appear became a running checkpoint in my psyche and altered the way I approached life. Unfortunately, this mentality also set a magnetic charge in my spirit that would draw events to me that supported this belief, so the story of struggling to find my inner peace began ... The more I struggled with trying to avoid freaky people and odd occurrences, the more I drew them to me! The more I tried to hide in the shadows from stressful situations, the more those situations hunted me down. Not understanding that I needed to face my fears and overcome them, I failed repeatedly and reinforced everything I so desperately wanted to avoid.

Where do I end and the rest of the world begin? How much control do I have over things that happen? How can I be sure bad things don't happen to me or around me? If you get what you focus on, then you can imagine the events that I drew to me with this as my focal point and primary question in life! Not only that, I expected perfection from myself. This unrealistic expectation set me up to be stressed over everything because if anything went wrong, I thought it was my fault.

During this time, I was a model at a local talent agency. Comparing myself to others, I always felt like the one who wasn't good enough to be there. I did get hired for jobs but looking at myself through the lens of every imperfection was harsh and I was young. I didn't know who I was and the constant comparison of myself to others made me unable to ever feel that my best was good enough. I became perfectionistic in every way and very hard on myself. Even though I knew all the modeling pictures were photo-shopped it didn't help my internal critic. I could follow a script and do as many takes as necessary until it was perfect, but I struggled to have a normal social conversation with anyone. All I knew how to do was work, at least, that's how it felt to me.

I developed an eating disorder that I later learned was a form of control for me. I basically quit eating. After a year of that habit, the anxiety was far worse because my poor body had nothing to work with to cope with the stress of daily life. I learned a lot recovering from that condition.

Rather than overcoming anxiety, I developed a "game face" version of myself that stepped forward to cover the internal geyser of stress and muffle the voice of doom.

The more I tried to control the environment, the more I blamed myself for everything that happened in my life or in the lives of others. This set me up to be easily manipulated and blamed by unhealthy people because it was already how I felt inside.

Looking back, fear was something my soul agreed to overcome. I was born feet first and blue. In the pictures I look like a tiny, petrified alien who was left here by accident by my people. The common theme in my life in one word can be summed up as "fear."

If I had a past life, I probably froze to death. I could have been hijacked by charismatic thugs. Perhaps I was hung for something I never said or possibly stoned to death because I got blamed for the downfall of the entire village. In school, whenever we studied slavery or the holocaust, I would dream that I was hiding in a wall, afraid to breathe or cough lest we would be found and sent to the gas chamber. I dreamed I was auctioned off in public and separated from my children. For the most part, I hid my sensitivity from those around me, trapped in my own little world of noticing everything while the big world I was forced to live in loomed above me... a tower of expectations that I had no desire to ever meet. Yet at the same time I had a connection to everything around me and deeper meanings that others didn't seem to have. If they did, they didn't discuss them anywhere in public where I could hear them.

I can say this about people with anxiety, and I feel I can speak as an expert because I was one of those people for most of my life – anxious people are actually quite gifted and sincere with a special empathic intelligence not recognized by the modern world. Anxious people have a very strong frequency that can be quite phenomenal at manifesting the object or event of their focus. Obviously, the goal is to change the focus so that you are bringing your highest and best potential into your life and not your deepest fear. However, even manifesting your deepest fear is a gift because it is an opportunity for you to face the dragon and conquer it. You never have to be afraid of it again! Anxious people have a high standard for themselves that needs a dose of self-love to balance it out.

Life is happening FOR you not TO you. Repeat this mantra as you become the main character in the movie about you overcoming anxiety. This is your movie. You are the hero. Everything that shows up in your movie is there so you can be the amazing main character you were created to be. Pretending I was in a movie really helped me respond differently to stress and maybe it will help you too. It's a lot more fun than being the extra in the corner hiding from the camera.

If you are a person reading this book because you have anxiety or you are in a relationship with someone who has anxiety issues, please be encouraged! Beneath that heart pounding, searing flood of high voltage energy is a Zen master – a finely tuned intuitive that has simply been repeatedly flattened by today's world and all the messages that go with it.

This book is about the one thing you can do something about. You! This journey is about getting in touch with the most powerful influence in your life and becoming some-one you love and admire. You can't do anything about a lot of things in this world. The one thing you can do something about is yourself. Don't ever give that power away! Knowing yourself and being in touch with what is you, and what is not you is the sword of truth in fighting the ghosts of anxiety inhabiting the halls of your house within. This book is going to help you tune your compass to true North and empower yourself to bring the life you were meant to live out of the shadows. The first thing you have to do is come home and live in the house of your spirit fully.

Learning to identify what feelings are yours and what you are picking up from the people around you is one of the keys to using your gift. Having a special intelligence and an empathic ability to tune in to those around you whether you like it or not is a challenging gift to have. Most people don't even know it's a gift until they stumble upon the information that gives them insight into this quality. Learning to work with it takes time and patience and an understanding of yourself and others that is worth the effort. In the meantime, being conscious that you are an antennae is important to remember. Otherwise, walking through a crowd of people can feel like riding on the end of an emotional yo-yo. To know what is not you or your energy, you have to be in touch with yourself to the core of your being. The first step is knowing what IS you!

Understanding how you are wired and how you intersect with the world around you is what this book is all about. The exercises are designed to help you look within and get a blueprint of what belongs in your life and supports your growth, and what needs to be eliminated. There are many suggestions to help you begin to create healthy boundaries. It is my desire that you can move from anxiety into joy and live the life you were created to experience.

You are also going to learn how to accept life on life's terms. You will grow in being able to handle whatever life throws at you because of a relationship you will develop with yourself built on love and trust. If you will follow the exercises and suggestions in this book and have patience with yourself, you really will feel better.

~ Holly Hudspeth

"It's not the event. It's what you do with it that determines the quality of your life."

– Tony Robbins

Chapter One

The Storage Room

"You find peace not by rearranging the circumstances of your life, but by realizing who you are at the deepest level."

– Eckhart Tolle

We are going to open the door and walk through the halls of anxiety, one room at a time. I will walk with you. As we turn on the lights, we will see the solutions waiting there that once cast a shadow on the walls, making the interior of this condition too frightening to face. These are your rooms, waiting to be reclaimed so you can once again come home and be comfortable in the house of your spirit. Having anxiety is like being haunted by a ghost that walks the halls of the house of your soul. As long as that ghost roams freely, you can never be truly relaxed. Even when you should feel safe at home, there is no rest because you never know... sometimes you have to wonder if the ghost in the halls is who you used to be, unable to live and yet not dead. You can and will escape from this condition and once again you can come back home to who you were created to be.

This is the beginning of your "welcome home" journey!

To begin, let's break through any negative beliefs you might have about yourself because of the anxiety that has inhabited your house without your consent. If you're going to break free and heal, you need to accept a few ideas before you will have the courage to move forward. There is nothing wrong with you. You are not broken. You are highly gifted but simply not trained to reach your potential. With a little insight you can and will redirect your energy and your focus to being who you were created to be without apology. So, without any further delay, let's begin the tour of the hallways and rooms of YOU! It's time to stop being homeless in the hallways of your life, missing out on who you could be because of what might be lurking around the next corner.

The first room we will enter as we walk through the hallway of anxiety is the storage room. You can visualize this room however you see fit. Maybe it looks like a garage or a room off the main entrance. However you want to see it is fine, just be aware that we are starting with the scariest room first so we can move you out of the past and into the present moment, then on to the future.

The storage room is where the past is stored and your perception of what happened in the past. This room is very powerful and often the one that drives our present moments and our decisions about the future. Most often it is in disarray and people want to avoid it. You walk through it daily without considering how a little organization could unleash a lot of energy that can be used in more productive ways. You could use it to create stability and a life you love, rather than a past you are trying to avoid recreating. It takes a lot of mental energy to avoid dealing with something every day. It's exhausting!

People love to say you cannot change the past and really that is a lie. We're going to accept that a lot of people say things that aren't really true all the time for various reasons and it's our job to begin to think about what we are told in a whole new way! We will decide for ourselves what is and will be our truth. That is deeply personal, and it seems messages everywhere are competing to tell us what is true and what is a lie. It can be overwhelming.

Sometimes the programming is just passed on from one generation to the next and we do not realize what they are saying is totally ridiculous. It is time to examine the stories we were told and also the stories we tell ourselves. The first step in taking your power back is to not take it personally; just go through the files of your mind and decide what to keep and what to pitch because it isn't serving your highest good.

As far as the past goes, how can we change it? We can change any memory by changing the meaning. What happened then is not how it is now and who we became as a result is right there in the mirror. We would not be ourselves today without every moment of our lives. Honor that truth.

We can also change the negative, unresolved memories that are still active in our minds. You will know what is active because when it crosses your mind it is in color and there is motion. You can smell the fresh rain or your grandmother's cookies baking. If you close your eyes and recall, it feels as if it is happening now. As those scenes replay your brain does not know the difference between what happened in the past and what is happening now. The chemical reaction in the brain and body is the same for the past and the present with these active memories. This is why visualization of your goals is so effective.

Any unresolved trauma is active in your memory and many times it drives our behavior and choices. That driver usually shows up to limit what we believe we should or must do to keep the event from happening again. It is called a limiting subconscious belief and in order to freely be ourselves, we must change them. The following exercise will help shift the subconscious beliefs by rewriting the past based on what we learned and who we have become as a result.

Trauma can come in any form and what is traumatic for me might not be traumatic for you. It is not fair to judge other people or even yourself for what ends up in your trauma files. We want to close them down properly, save them in our brain and claim the gift that came with them. This is powerful and life changing.

Leave your judgement at the door. Deciding if events should have happened or blaming yourself has no place here. You did the best you could in any situation as did the other people involved. Maybe you do not think your best was good enough. That is not for you to say. What is for you to say, in a loving fashion, is that you did the best you could and accept that in your heart.

Everything turned out okay because you are here reading this book and that means there is always another moment to make a better choice and express yourself differently. Releasing regret helps us avoid repeating the memory. To do that you must accept that you did the best you could at that time. Love yourself enough to give yourself as much credit as possible with your memories.

Make a list of the traumatic events in your life. These events caused you to create a file of things you'll avoid to protect yourself. For instance, if you dated a soccer player with dark hair who was short, had a bulldog and cheated on you, the file becomes, "do not date the following people: short men, men with bulldogs, men with dark hair, men who play sports." You can see how this is not any kind of safety net in life, yet our brain still attempts to make sense of traumatic events and flag any conditions that can be flagged in order to ensure this never happens again.

If you are a sensitive person and events really affected you from a young age, then your file will become significant by the time you are in college. Before too long, you really become the person who has control issues! Whether you realize it or not, there are more things you cannot do than things you can do on your list. At that point life gets pretty miserable and you are too young to live like that regardless of your actual age. This exercise will reclaim the parts of yourself that were lost in those events and add to your spirit the wisdom you need to know you can handle life. You will be more creative and loving, more open and free after completing this exercise. I say this because it is true and also to encourage you. Trauma rewires the brain. Our brains want to connect, and trauma causes the brain to want to protect. If you want to have good relationships in life, healing the trauma will allow you to connect to the people around you.

Sit with your list in front of you. Be aware that within each of those events there is a version of you that is still there, unable to move forward until he or she is freed from the continuous loop of the repeating story in your mind. This means that not only have you lost a part of yourself, but that part is trapped at that age until you come as the healer and liberator. This exercise is an amazing act of self-love and takes you from being the victim to the hero of your own story. It also closes the trauma file on that event and allows your brain to make meaning and store the event in the past where it belongs!

You can expect to have a lot more energy after doing this exercise because the human brain uses more energy than most of the other systems in the body and it will run unresolved files endlessly until you shut them down. The brain also cannot tell the difference between what we imagine and what we are actually experiencing, so when we have bad memories that replay and replay, the impact of an event is multiplied as if it happened every day for months or even years. You can see why taking the time to do this is vitally important and a huge game changer in how we feel each day.

Take an event on the list you feel confident about stepping into. If need be, choose a smaller one at first so you can see how this works without freaking yourself out. Mentally see yourself as being surrounded by your angels or spirit guides or ancestors. Become aware that there is a host of witnesses in the spirit realm who are supporting your growth and they will be with you to cheer you on as you revisit this memory. Step into the memory and smell, taste, feel the moment either before or after the event occurred. I like to go in after because that version of myself is usually vulnerable, available and seeking comfort.

As you step into the memory, see it in motion and color, but freeze everything in the scene except yourself. Make everything in the scene black and white but you at whatever age you were. You are in color and moving. Stand before that version of you and hold out your hand. Hold the child if you were a child. Touch yourself and dry your tears. Tell that version of you how everything is going to be okay. Tell yourself it works for the good and that you are learning and growing from this situation. Feel the love you have for yourself in that moment with the wisdom you have all these years later.

Look around the black and white scene for a gift. When you get to it, open the gift and see what's inside. Celebrate what your spirit gained from this experience! This is a gift for life. It may be compassion or wisdom or a number of other things, but it is a part of your story and it is to be embraced because without it you wouldn't be who you are today and who you are is good.

As you embrace that version of you, allow that "you" to reunite with your spirit. Reclaim that person instead of leaving them in the horrible replaying memory. As you leave, you are going to mark this file as inactive in your brain. It goes into the "past" filing cabinet. To do so, you will make the scene become black and white like a photograph and put it behind you. Take the door of that room, close it behind you and lock it. Put the key in your pocket and know that you can revisit that room whenever you need to and only when you intend to do so.

The person you were at that point is now reintegrated into your spirit and healed. You have begun the process of owning your story as an overcomer rather than an unhealed victim! Because of that your spirit is stronger. Take a moment to breathe deeply and recognize how the memory and the story have changed.

Do this exercise as many times as you need to and begin to develop a new relationship with yourself based on respect and trust. Your memories are becoming events that you handled and whatever comes your way, you can and will handle it. Instead of being ashamed and afraid, you are becoming strong and proud. The past will be something that happened, not something that happened to you that can never happen again because you barely made it through and you're dangling by a thread.

Be aware that there is an emotional cleanse that happens when you begin this process. You might sleep more or less than usual. You might laugh more or cry more depending on what your spirit needs in order to balance. Trust yourself with this process and embrace the changes within you. If you are ravenously hungry, then eat good food. If you want to be alone and reconnect with yourself then honor that. Remember this is a process and the more you allow the process, the faster it will resolve into a brave new life for you and everyone you love. The person you will love the most will be you! Instead of being afraid of yourself, you will be your own best friend. You are becoming free to enjoy the adventure of life knowing you can always count on yourself to love you and understand you and accept you for the rest of your life.

The other aspect of an emotional cleanse is understanding that emotions are stored in the cells of our body and when the memories become inactive, the body releases the old energy that accompanied the memory. Drinking a lot of clean, structured water is a good idea. Structured water is water as it naturally forms on earth. Think spring water and mineral water. Non-structured water is water that has been distilled. It helps flush the system of the old and that is what we are doing – releasing the old! Natural spring water is the best choice for reloading your cells with hydration that is grounded in the movement of the Earth's energy. It is a stable form of water and since a large portion of your body is made of water this is your best option. Being conscious of this emotional flush is a very mindful and empowering way to bring what is happening in your mind and spirit into the physical world. Drinking water is a healthy and easy habit to support the process of cleansing things that no longer serves you.

Herbal organic teas are also great in aiding the nervous system and body during this time of reclaiming yourself and cleansing traumatic memories. I find the Organic India Tulsi teas to be extraordinary due to the holy basil herb which is an elixir of the nervous system. Allow yourself time to sleep during this time because our brains cleanse themselves while we sleep. Closing down active files allows your brain to discard a lot of energy stealing thoughts during sleep.

You will be rewarded with an intense sense of calm and well-being upon awakening. It is very refreshing compared to the impending doom of past anxiousness. Keep notes in your journal about your dreams and experiences as you wake up to the current moment without the past always there to warn you about making the same mistake again. Closing those trauma files creates a new conversation with yourself about life that is positive and full of potential. Everything in this world longs to grow! We are all wired for growth and life, allowing that to come forth without fear is a wonderful new place to be. Embrace the shift.

We are moving from the anguish of the past to tools you can use in the present moment for redirecting anxiety before it overwhelms you. Make it a point to use these tools daily.

Chapter Two

The Toolbox

"We need to look at our mind, body and emotions as tools. We own them. They don't own us."

– Dandapani

In the storage room we're going to look in the toolbox for some items you can put in your pocket as you walk through the hallways in the house of your stress, anxiety and panic. These items will be useful to remember and can bring you back to a calm place very quickly. These ideas will best serve you if you make them into habits for the duration of this journey. Many people keep these tools as habits for a healthy and balanced life.

Be aware that if you have been anxious for a long time, the cells and thinking patterns you have conditioned yourself to will try to conform back to anxious patterns. This is like muscle memory in sports or any other athletic training where you have repeated the same movement until it is memorized. The pattern of habitual anxiety must be broken and retraining yourself is part of this process.

If you sense anxiety rising out of habit, use some of the tools in this book to allow it to pass and replace the anxious thoughts with enthusiasm for the future you are headed toward. No longer will you be held hostage by anxious thinking! Replace the anxious thought with a happy thought, quote or vision. Remember, you are retraining your brain and the brain is a muscle. It's worth the work and you won't be sorry when the habit is broken. Tony Robbins has a great retraining exercise for anxious thinking. He recommends asking yourself, "What's great about this?" whenever a stressful situation occurs. Any time you ask yourself a question, you will answer it. If you ask better questions in life, you will get better answers. The next time you feel an anxious response to life's stress, ask yourself what's great about this and watch how differently you respond to the situation! It might even make you laugh out loud to hear the answer you give yourself.

One of the best tools you have for breaking the chains of anxiety is right between your ears. The very thing that is causing the problem is a massive key to the solution. The simple but profound truth is that your brain is the best thing you have going for you in ending anxiety. Every day learn something new. When you learn new things, your brain builds new neural pathways creating an endorphin rush making you happy. It is impossible to have anxiety when you are actively engaged in new information that excites you. Find something you are interested in and learn about it in a way you enjoy with a teacher you admire. Make time to explore this new subject or activity every day.

Taking some time during the day to put your bare feet in the ground and touch your skin to the Earth is also tremendously important. The Earth has a magnetic field that grounds energy. We are energetic beings. Emotions and memories and thoughts have an energy too. Standing with your feet on the earth will stabilize you and release that nervous and spastic energy into the Earth's field. This will balance your physical and mental systems.

This is one more empowering action you can take to reclaim who you are and what you are here to do now. You are here for a purpose and that purpose is to thrive. Release the barely hanging on old pattern into the Earth. Many generations of people have walked that same ground and they all had many moments and thoughts and feelings too. Allow that awareness to strengthen you, knowing that this moment will pass. Each day you are becoming a person who owns every moment of your life. You are stretching into a person who will dream big dreams of a future you are very capable of handling.

Plan things to look forward to. Not only will you make great memories, but you will also have a focal point for the future that brings you joy. Any time you are having anxiety about the future, you can move to the anticipation of the plans you have that are rooted in pleasure. It is also a way to get your power back and begin to take control of your life.

There are stones that carry a grounding energy such as hematite, tourmaline, smoky quartz, and petrified wood. These stones carry a frequency that stabilizes the energy we have in our bodies and even helps our thoughts to move into a grounded signal instead of one that ricochets around in our mental and physical fields. I wear bracelets made of these stones and you can choose a stone for your pocket or bracelet or pendant to wear. This can aid you in the process of getting your energy stable. If nothing else, these stones are a reminder to release any stress you are feeling into the Earth and not hold your stress inside where it can keep you anxious. Holding the stress and anxiety inside is part of what allows it to roam the halls of your house and return later to haunt what should be a good time. We don't want to leave that in the house. Return it to the Earth in a proper burial so your house can be full of life.

Becoming aware of yourself, the thought patterns you are holding, and breaking that habit of anxious patterns is the first step to getting your life back. When I first started this exercise, I would be aware of the anxious energy and release it with breath and feel myself like a tree with roots deep in the Earth. This mental image calmed me and replaced the thought I didn't want to be having. It allowed me to be in charge of what my mind was going to think about. I went from being tormented by my thoughts to being calmed by them. It was empowering to be in control of my state of being with just one mental image.

I also took charge of my day before putting my feet on the floor in the morning. I would get centered in my spirit and come to a place of understanding that life is happening for me, not to me. Everything is for my good and I have everything I need within me. No matter what happens today, I will handle it with grace and ease. I set my focus to look for the good and wonderful things happening for me and around me. Changing your focus is one of the biggest shifts you can make. Remember, we see what we are looking for whether it is in the grocery store or in life. Look for the good. Look for opportunity to do good. How can you contribute to the world around you today?

Find someone who has an ambitious and worthwhile goal and offer to help them achieve that goal. Volunteer somewhere to help people or animals in a way that is meaningful to you. This helps put your own life into perspective as well as bringing a feeling of significance that supports positive growth. Positive, purpose-driven growth crowds out anxious feelings.

Stop talking about your anxiety. Talk about your hopes, dreams and ambitions. Share what you have learned in your personal growth and development. Laugh. Talk about what inspires and drives others. Move anxiety off the main topic of conversation. We get what we focus on and we create with our words. Begin to create what you want, not what you want to avoid.

Move! Make movement a part of your day. Whether it's stretching, walking or dance, moving is beneficial for relaxation and release of stress. It allows us to be seated firmly in our physical body and own that space. Most of us aren't moving enough. Some of the roots of anxiety happen because we are not letting go of excess energy physically every day. Mentally we can be exhausted because we sit, dwell, worry and think too much. Taking a walk or stretching quickly moves you into a different space.

If you are having emotions you feel anxious about, make time to sit with each feeling as it comes up. Observe it. Talk to it. Ask the pain or sorrow or guilt what it is here to teach you. When we have emotions we don't like, we try to block them. We fear them and experience an anxious state because we do not like what we are feeling. The truth is, feelings change when we sit with them as a teacher. Acknowledging the feelings and observing the lesson changes the dynamic between you and your emotions. It opens the flow of energy so the emotion passes through without getting trapped. Avoiding the feeling only gives it more power. There is no need to hide from your feelings. Allow them to speak and teach and you will become stronger and wiser as a result.

Plan your time. Plan your days for a reasonable amount of activities and give yourself time to live your life at a natural pace. If you are rushing all day every day, then something needs to go. Be the master of your time; don't fall into the trap that being faster is better. Working harder is sometimes just working harder. There is a natural pace that works for your life; you can operate at this pace and feel good. Find it and begin to slow down or speed up according to what you need.

Another great way to restore calmness is to rub your hands together to create energy, then cup them over your eyes so it's dark. The energy generated from your hands and the darkness is an instant reset for your nervous system. This is something you can do when a breathing exercise isn't a great option. You can experiment and see what solutions work best for you.

An exercise that is calming and healing for the nervous system is to engage in an activity where you are very focused and in the moment. During these activities, your perception of time is different. If you don't have the time and space to do that, you can focus on a small object and notice the details of that object. This engages a different part of your brain and brings your nervous system back to a place of calm, focused control.

Self-talk is a massive tool in your toolbox! What you say to yourself is very important. Really becoming aware of how you talk to yourself can be shocking if you step back and observe the messages you tell yourself day after day. Whatever you say to yourself will be considered true in your brain. This can work for you or against you depending on what you are saying. If you want to feel better, you must coach yourself to handle life's disappointments and setbacks. Encourage yourself and be a good friend to yourself in your own mind. Changing the things you say to yourself when things aren't going the way you would like is going to improve everything for you. Be aware and be positive. I can't stress this enough.

Keep these tools handy and use them. With these tools, you can begin to repave, remodel and rebuild the halls and walls of your house of spirit. To be free of the chilling ghosts of anxiety, you need to be fully present and taking ownership of yourself and your life.

So let's move on to everyone's favorite room in the house....

Chapter Three

The Kitchen

"One cannot think well, love well, sleep well,
if one has not dined well."

– Virginia Woolf

While anxiety is a deeply personal condition, all anxiety doesn't come from inside us. The first culprit we are going to look at causes a lot of anxiety in a place you might not think to look. Food is supposed to sustain us, comfort us and nourish us. Not all food works for all people. We are individuals inside and out; that includes what diet is ideal for you.

We are going to explore some dietary issues that can cause anxiety. While people with food allergies are often aware of their allergy, people who are sensitive to foods can have symptoms they might not correlate to food right away. If you eat something and it makes your stomach hurt, you will most likely know something you ate caused the pain. Other symptoms of food allergies can be more elusive, and anxiety CAN be a side effect of a diet that isn't working for you.

Doing this exercise requires patience and diligence. If you are suffering from extreme anxiety, you are probably willing to try anything, and that type of dedication ultimately leads to success. Keeping a food journal is a MUST because some food items do not aggravate the system until the second day after they are assimilated into the body. Let's face it, you often do not remember what you had for lunch yesterday and certainly will not remember if you are under a lot of stress (because of what stress does to the brain – but we will cover that in the next chapter).

Keep a small journal with you at all times and write down what you eat and drink all day. Many people are dehydrated and believe they are drinking water. Once you start keeping a journal, you'll become aware that what you think is going on is not really accurate. Also, keeping a food journal helps you to be mindful of making better choices because you are recording your activity and writing 'salad' on the line feels pretty good.

The first day or two, write down your activity and get used to keeping track of what you are eating and drinking and also how you are feeling. If you are happy, depressed, anxious or restless, make a note of those feelings. What we eat and drink is often mood-altering. Noticing that you are a human teeter-totter because of sugar or artificial dyes can really help motivate you to make a dietary change! The goal is to have better days and better relationships with yourself and others.

After a few days of journaling, you can begin to know how to make better choices. Hopefully, the journal exercise is eye-opening and inspiring to you. You can approach it as something that is fun and different. You might just stumble upon the missing link to your sanity along the way!

To start with, add fresh, organic food into your diet. Whatever time of day you are most likely to feel over-whelmed is the starting point for you. If you hit a stress point at 3 pm, make sure your lunch is fresh and organic. Pesticides cause a lot of damage to the nervous system and eliminating them from one meal a day will quickly convert you to a believer in organic foods. Fresh foods contain photon energy from the sun and our bodies thrive on photon energy! Photons support all our energy systems. They are easy for the body to convert into the necessary nutrients and they also cleanse many other toxins that could be aggravating your nervous system (such as heavy metals).

Consume as many root vegetables as possible. Please make sure they are organic, as root vegetables can be very toxic if they have been exposed to pesticides. Sweet potatoes, beets, carrots and any other vegetable that grows under the Earth is a root vegetable. These tubers are very supportive, grounding and full of minerals. You want a deep root into the Earth in order to be stable and solid. Eating the vegetable that is a picture of stability is immensely helpful! You will notice a difference right away.

Beets, carrots and sweet potatoes can be roasted in olive oil with garlic and Himalayan salt. This is a great comfort food; it is filling and pushes you toward your goal of being anxiety free. If you approach your food as either being a solution or a problem, it will help you make better choices and heal the nervous system more quickly.

Carrots, beets, green apples, and celery can also be juiced. If you do not like cooked root vegetables, then try juicing them! While I do not recommend juicing a potato, I will say beets, carrots and green apples complement each other very well and can be readily absorbed into your bloodstream in fresh juice form. This is an energy burst your body will love and a habit you will not be willing to give up. There are many fresh juice bars now as their popularity grows and if you feel an urge, you can get your own juicer. I recommend the Breville cold-pressed juicer – it is easy to clean and inexpensive, plus it makes fast work of juicing.

Avoid processed foods; this includes things that come in a box, things that have a lot of dye and anything you need to put in the microwave. Artificial dyes are very, very harmful to the nervous system and many are made from chemicals no person should ever eat! Taking yourself off these foods for a few weeks and keeping a journal is a good way to see who you are without these poisons. You might find that you are a very calm and happy person without the help of red dye #40 to distort your perception of reality. How would that distort your perception of reality? Because at the core it is a poison, and the body has a panic response to being poisoned. If you are having anxiety and there is not an external factor to explain why you feel that way, the anxiety signal could be coming from inside your body because it is being overloaded with toxins.

Aspartame is another big bad ugly for the nervous system. Made from parasite excrement, aspartame causes a lot of side effects that can ruin your life. Read labels and avoid it at all costs. It's not worth it!!!

After a week of drinking plenty of water, eating fresh foods and root vegetables daily, and a glass of fresh juice – look at your food journal and your moods. How is your sleep? How is your anxiety? If you are still having extreme anxiety, the next item to eliminate as a potential culprit is gluten.

People are often sensitive or allergic to gluten. The number of people with gluten sensitivities is growing because wheat in the United States now has a genetic modification with 14 biomarkers in it that are identical to human blood. Long story short, your body uploads it as a different substance than what it is. Gluten ends up in the body where it does not need to be and causes a whole lot of problems along the way. Grains are also heavily sprayed with pesticides during growing and after harvest.

Anxiety is very commonly triggered by gluten and many people who have celiac disease spend time in a psychiatric ward before being properly diagnosed; gluten was causing their issues, not a mental disorder. Needless to say, this traumatic experience only made their anxiety worse.

Removing gluten from the diet has an almost immediate resolution to the panic, anxiety and stress coming from the body's warning signals. Remember, gluten is toxic for gluten-intolerant people and deadly to those with celiac disease.

Many stores have gluten free products; choose those if you do not want to give up bread and pasta. Going gluten free is only effective if you try it for a few weeks because the first week of giving up gluten will be an adjustment. If gluten is causing you problems, you will notice feeling less anxious, but there is a little balancing act involved in giving it up. Just be aware not to get stuck feeling sorry for yourself when you go gluten free. Find restaurants and grocery store products that are gluten free beforehand so you can still enjoy the things you love to eat. This is a discovery, not a punishment.

Keep being mindful of your state of mind and your sleep (record them in your journal) and soon you will see a picture of what foods help you and what foods harm you.

Finding out what works for your body is not a formula someone can give you. It's not a pre-packaged diet plan. It is discovering and honoring who you are as an individual and consuming the best fuel to get the best result. No food item is worth having a panic attack. No beverage or snack is worth having sweaty palms and wondering if you can trust yourself not to tailspin into an anxious moment in front of your friends and family.

Here is a list of other food items that can cause or aggravate anxiety:

- grains
- corn
- dairy
- alcohol
- sugar
- artificial dyes
- artificial sweeteners
- caffeine
- pasta
- pesticides
- GMO crops
- high fructose corn syrup
- soda
- diet soda
- white bread
- energy drinks
- soy processed foods

If you want to keep it simple and not have to think about it too much, you can approach it like this: eat only organic food and that includes beverages and snacks. Have a fresh salad and fresh juice every day. Avoid gluten. Don't drink any sodas or foods that have dyes. Protein needs to be grass-fed organic if its animal protein. Drink more water! Snacks need to be healthy foods like dried fruits and nuts or veggie sticks. Eat less sugar and absolutely NO artificial sweeteners. Branch out and try new recipes. Try more mushrooms. Mushrooms are super healthy, and they also pull a lot of unwanted toxins out of your body. Just remember, every bite of food is either moving you toward your goal or pushing you back into a place you don't want to be. Feeling good is its own reward. If a food item makes you feel strange, anxious and unsettled, then stop eating it.

Look into the superfoods that support healthy energy. These include many types of sprouts, organic dark green leafy vegetables, organic berries, green tea, moringa tea, spirulina powder, maca powder and many more. The powders can be added to smoothies to support your mind and body with a solid energy throughout the day and without a crash factor.

Probiotics are also absolutely essential to having a healthy response to stress. Most people do not have the right amount of probiotics, or healthy bacteria in their digestive tract. Antibiotics, pesticides, heavy metals and processed foods kill that healthy flora and cause problems not just in your digestive tract, but also in your brain. All the neurotransmitters in your brain are created in your digestive tract and when the brain needs them, they serve the higher function of helping thoughts happen. If these probiotics are missing from your digestive tract, then it isn't functioning properly to make the neurotransmitters. That means when the brain calls for them, they are not there. The brain's job is to wire and fire thoughts; when it can't perform this function it sends a signal that something is missing, something is wrong. This signal is often translated into anxiety. The anxious person is looking at their life in the moment and wondering, "Why am I panicking when nothing is wrong that I can see?"

Something is wrong... inside. The brain and heart are closely connected; when the brain struggles the heart responds. While we do not know for sure that the heart creates emotion it definitely is a conduit. Humans say it is beating with joy, heavy with sorrow, in your throat and down at your toes. The heart will often step in to assist when the brain is struggling, creating an emotional response to what was a thought-based issue.

This can cause an anxious, overly emotional response to life's simple problems. This response turns into negative thoughts of wondering what is wrong with you and why everyone else is not as upset as you by the same situation. Needless to say, this form of alienation only further exacerbates the anxiety you are already feeling. The solution is biological. Help your body get what it needs to perform its designated function. The alienation of feeling like you live in an alternate reality can end and the emotional response to mental stress will be alleviated. This will give you extra energy each day to create a life you love living.

If you have taken many antibiotics or eaten the foods named above, getting a lot of good probiotics in your system will help tremendously and change your life! If you were not breastfed as a baby this is particularly important because the original seeding of your digestive tract was not in place. For these people, probiotics are even more important and create an even more noticeable change.

Probiotic supplements can be purchased. In my opinion, the best way to bring them in is via food, such as miso soup, kefir, kombucha, sauerkraut, and yogurt. If you did not get colostrum (from your mother's milk) as a baby, you might want to use a supplement and all these foods intensely for 30 days. Probiotics aren't something you will take for just awhile. In the polluted world we live in, probiotics are a necessity and should become part of your daily routine indefinitely.

A good, organic, food-based multivitamin with minerals is also essential to having a happy and balanced life. Having low iron or low B complex vitamins alters your nervous system's ability to function. That can result in you wondering what is wrong with your mood, your outlook on life and mental function. Minerals are imperative for brain cognition and many mental disturbances are caused by a mineral deficiency. Minerals come from the soil and they act as energy conduits in the human body. Without minerals, the exchange of energy is not regulated properly which results in either not enough exchange or too much. Without minerals, your body cannot unlock energy systems and get what it needs to function properly. Since the soil in our country is depleted of minerals, my recommendation is a mineral rich, organic, food-derived liquid vitamin supplement taken in the morning. Food-based supplements are best because they deliver vitamins and minerals in a structured form your body can recognize. When cooking, use sea salt or Himalayan salt. Adding sea salt to your bath is a great way for your body to uptake minerals from the water.

Something else to consider is magnesium. Magnesium deficiency is very common in the United States. A lack of magnesium can cause poor sleep, muscle cramps and anxiety. Magnesium deficiency makes feet stink and causes some forms of body odor. Epsom salt baths are the best way to alleviate this. Soaking before bed for longer than 20 minutes is necessary for your body to absorb the magnesium. Magnesium body spray is sold at health food stores; spritzing it on your skin will help your body absorb it throughout the day. These are such simple ideas but absolutely vital for your body to function properly. If you are not adding them to your diet or supplementing, then you have a deficiency and correcting that will feel like a miracle to your body and your mind.

Another key factor that people often don't think about is brain food. Healthy fats are vital for a calm, functioning brain. Be sure to eat plenty of grass-fed butter, organic olive oil, walnuts, avocados and coconut oil. All these healthy fats feed the mitochondrial function in your brain and they have a focused, calming effect that I think you will notice and enjoy. If you feed your brain what it needs, the effect is more balanced mental clarity and more overall confidence in problem-solving and goal-setting. You will have more energy and feel better. You will perform better in school and life will be easier.

Now that you have new dietary options to explore and new information to consider, do not forget to plan meals and fun events surrounding this culinary adventure. Try new recipes with friends. Plan meals with people you love. You can include your friends and keep a food journal together. Make the food journaling a mindful, intentional, wonderful new chapter in your life. Remember that learning new things is a key to breaking anxious thinking! Cooking is tactile and very engaging. Be creative in your exploration of which foods work for you and inspire others to join you! You never know what opportunities can come from this part of your journey with the right attitude applied in the kitchen. Be open to new and amazing moments. Involve your friends! Culturally, food is social. Looking up recipes and cooking with your friends is a fun way to explore how food affects you.

Now, grab a snack and enter the room where the party is…

Chapter Four

The Den

"Stop giving other people the power to control your happiness and your mind, and your life.
If you don't take control of yourself and your own life, someone else is bound to try."

– Roy T. Bennett, *The Light in the Heart*

Next on our list of rooms in the hallway is the family room or den. This is the room where you watch television, movies, get on social media and spend time with people you do life with. We need to look at the people around you and the images you are putting in your head.

We will start with the people first. Usually people with anxiety have a difficult time with boundaries. This is because anxious people don't even trust themselves and the world is an unstable and unpredictable place. Figuring out the who and what of things can be confusing when anxiety is a constant companion. Toxic people love anxious people because it is easy to blame a person with anxiety! Anxious people commonly think everything is their fault anyway, or at least feel they could have done something to avoid it.

Usually, anxious people are a dream come true for toxic people because they are easily manipulated, and they have a high degree of compassion. People with anxiety will drop everything to help another person and listen to someone's repetitive problems for as long as necessary, because they really need to feel they are making a difference in this world. Sometimes just listening to someone else talk about their problems makes the anxious person feel better about their own life. This can sometimes be empowering because even if you cannot fix your own anxiety, you can help your friend have a better day. Anxiety and panic erode your self-worth. One way of feeling worthy is to help another person.

This can become a problem when friendships become a dumping ground and the anxious person takes it all in like a landfill. Your world is composed of the people in it. Your reality is defined by the day to day events, the people and the stories you consume. When your phone is full of calls and texts from people freaking out about life and every moment is a dramatic event, the tipping point can become a slippery slope. Remember, you are a sensitive being. That sensitivity is part of how you ended up in this position. Instead of hating yourself for being sensitive or feeling weak, it is time to see it as a gift. So, what's great about being an empathic, sensitive person?

For starters, sensitive people pick up on things before they happen. They notice the moods and emotions of others in such a way that they are easy people to have a relationship with if you respect their sensitivity. Sensitive people care about what happens in the world around them; they care about the people in their world. They can be very supportive and loving. Many sensitive people have a healing gift or a spiritual gift. They often have a keen appreciation for good music, good food, animals and nature. When they have time to reflect and be calm, they often have brilliant solutions to problems that can help a great number of people.

If you are a sensitive person, camping out in misery with your friend is agonizing! Not only do you take in all that negative energy, but if your friend is determined to be miserable, they will drag you into their darkness. Being a loyal and loving sensitive person with anxiety issues, this poses a real problem because you can't leave them in their misery, but you can't fix it for them either.

Your friends appreciate being able to share their pain because, whether you know it or not, you are taking their misery from them and ingesting it. They feel better without having to change, and many times become dependent on you to take their pain and give them love in return.

This type of relationship is harmful to a sensitive soul because it pushes down on their energy systems and causes more anxiety by providing evidence that the world is a scary and dangerous place. There is a feedback loop between what you believe and what shows up. Panic, stress, and worry have thoughts and memories attached to them. Those energy patterns attract their reflection into your life to support what you believe. When the reflection shows up, it validates the belief and the feedback loop goes on.

If you want to break the chains of anxiety, you have to change not only what you believe, but the people in your life. Begin looking for friends who are confident and successful so you can watch and learn from them. Being sensitive, you will pick up on their energy and they will lift you up; it is the same type of transfer that allowed negative people to pull you down. Wouldn't you rather be uplifted?

The key to being a healthy sensitive person is to use the gift of sensitivity to empower yourself. Then you can empower others to be the best version of themselves by honoring their unique gifts and talents. This means seeing people as contagious. You have to crawl out from under anxiety through your own choice and everyone around you will have to deal with their own life circumstances as well. From now on when the drama people call, set a timer for five minutes. When you answer them via phone or text you let them know you only have a minute, but you wanted to answer because you care about them. Offer your support in the form of a solution they can choose to utilize and let them know you will get back with them later. They will either use the solution you gave them or contact someone else to dwell in their misery until you are available. We become like the people we spend time with. Find people you want to be like; they have qualities and talents you would like to have. Spend time with these people, learn from them and watch your life grow as a result.

Eventually you will see a pattern with these people. As you make healthy choices and roll up your sleeves to get your own life under control, they will either be growing with you or you will grow apart. It will happen organically as a natural by-product of your growth. If they need to go, allowing them to do so is a drama-free way to keep moving forward in your life without any additional trauma, stress and anxiety.

"Stories you read when you're the right age never quite leave you. You may forget who wrote them or what the story was called. Sometimes you'll forget precisely what happened, but if a story touches you it will stay with you, haunting the places in your mind that you rarely ever visit."

– Neil Gaiman, *M is for Magic*

Now, let us examine what you are taking into your being through media, whether that is social media, television, movies, music... etc. Remember when I talked about your mind not knowing the difference between a past memory and what is happening now? When you take in entertainment, news, music or anything that offers a visual or auditory signal, there is often an emotional response on your part that goes with it. Time spent here often seems relaxing and idle, but it is actually very interactive on your part because your brain is signaling your body, responding to what it sees. You must be very careful what you take in if you are trying to heal from anxiety issues. The rule is NO NEW DAMAGE!

Social media and anything that causes you to compare yourself to other people needs to be eliminated. Either stop comparing yourself or stop looking at it. Everyone has something in their life that they struggle with no matter how rich, famous or beautiful they are. Understanding that is part of maturity and intelligence. If you're feeling bad looking at what other people are doing, stop!!! Start creating things for yourself to do that make you happy. Use the time you were spending comparing yourself to others to start building yourself into the person you want to be.

Focus on things that lift you up, calm you or make you grateful and happy. Anything that evokes fear, worry, sadness, grief and hysteria should be strictly avoided for at least 30 days. Your body is purging old memories, food toxins and coming into a place of rebalancing. You cannot determine what is helping or healing your anxiety if you are getting upset by politics, the injustices of the world or horror movies. Your nervous system is a sensitive place and in order to sort it out and become a calm and well-adjusted person, you have to stop allowing external images and opinions to throw your emotions all over the map. Listen to music that is happy or calming.

You can find meditation music on the internet that is encoded with HRZ frequencies that affect every cell in your body to bring healing and inner peace. Draw, paint, go hiking, meditate; just take a break from all the ways media is sending you fear, panic or any other feeling they choose. This is a time for you to get in touch with yourself and where your feelings are coming from; to do that you have to draw a distinct line between me and not me. So, be aware of what you are allowing into your psyche and how long you let it stay there. Anything that enters is something you will have to sort out mentally so only take in those ideas and stories that support your journey and lift you up.

Give yourself a much-needed break from the bombardment of messages we receive daily. Social media can go on without you for a month. When you go back you will be different, but the news media will not have changed. The difference is that when you go back, you will see the messages of fear and anxiety and you will not be so easily played after you have had time to heal.

I think people often overlook the fact that the brain is a consumer as well as a producer. This is true not only of media, but many other forms of intake for the brain you might not have considered. The brain feeds on healthy fat and is a part of the nervous system. Your eyes are the only part of your brain that sit outside the skull and they highly influence the activity of the nervous system. What type of light and how much you are taking in through your eyes plays a vital role in your brain activity and energy level. We need sunlight during the day and total darkness at night. Even a small amount of light coming from an electronic device can disturb the production of vital secretions your body makes while you sleep. Without the proper balance, your performance during the day will be affected as will your ability to confidently move through the waking hours.

The brain consumes a lot of the energy you take in from healthy fats such as olive oil, coconut oil and avocados. It needs this fuel to function. The brain is also taking in what you see and responding to that visual stimuli in a number of ways. If you are having stress and anxiety issues, use your brain to your advantage by consuming calming images and pleasant scenes.

Being in a relaxed state several times throughout the day is very important for brain function. When the fight or flight response kicks in, the body moves into a different mode where energy is conserved and channeled to the systems that keep you alive in a high combat or running scenario. We all know that. What a lot of people do not consider is that while the body is directing energy toward fight or flight, it is not using energy for other vital functions.

Digestion is compromised, meaning vitamins and minerals are not properly absorbed. Any detoxification the body might need to do for general housekeeping is "denied. The body will not use energy to heal if it feels you are under direct threat. The brain locks and energy is directed to the frontal lobe. This means access to other parts of your brain is not available. A great example of this is when a talented student has testing anxiety and cannot remember anything during the test, but afterward can tell you everything that was on it with clarity.

If you are in a state of perpetual stress and don't move to the relaxed mode, this state becomes a lifestyle. Then it is like the gas pedal gets stuck in super stress mode. This is how chronic stress becomes anxiety and then develops into anxiety attacks and panic attacks. Besides being debilitating to your relationship with yourself, others and life, it is also very physically damaging and leads to other, more serious health issues that can become chronic.

So, what does a lifestyle of stress overload do to your body and why is it a problem? Stress and anxiety are issues because the body is redirecting energy causing your systems to get out of balance. Toxins, inflammation and pain build up, vitamin and mineral levels destabilize, and you do not even have access to your wisdom and creative problem-solving abilities. Not only that, the body needs minerals so badly, it will begin to load heavy metals and toxins into your bones or anything that remotely looks like what its receptors need. Toxins build up the same way trash does in a warzone. You cannot take it out of your house because there is a battle going on outside. It is not long before your house is a mess.

This is one way chronic stress becomes anxiety which becomes panic. Your body is screaming at you to relax. There has to be a balance to all things and the human body is no exception. If we don't honor the balance, we get symptoms. Symptoms are the body's way of asking for what it needs. If you just take a pill to mask the symptoms, then the problem escalates until you become ill and are forced to rest and put the world in its place so your body can heal. It isn't necessary to take it that far if you understand how you are made and honor that. The reward is creating a balanced life you love and feeling a sense of calm and well-being.

Speaking of calm, let's move to the room of total rest...

Chapter Five

The Bedroom

*"Now I see the secret of making the
best person: it is to grow in the open air and
to eat and sleep with the Earth."*

– Walt Whitman

The next room we have in the hallway of your house is the bedroom. Your bedroom should be a calm and relaxing place for resting. It is not an office, movie theatre or a storage space. It is the sanctuary where you dream and sleep and heal.

Going to sleep is an art form. Falling asleep well becomes the beginning of the next day. This is the day you will begin when you wake up. Taking time before bed to make a list of things you will deal with in the morning helps clear the mind. Deep breathing exercises help set the tone for resting time. When you exhale longer than you inhale, it sends a message to your body that everything is calm. So, inhale for a five-count, hold your breath for a five-count and exhale for eight seconds. Do this three times in a row and feel your heart rate slow. Start with the bottom of your feet and mentally release the stress from your body working your way to the top of your head. Everything you think about gives a command to your body. Now it is time to rest, dream and heal.

When you sleep the brain cleans itself. It removes any plaque and regenerates. The kidneys, liver, gallbladder and other purifying organs clean themselves as well. Sleeping properly is worth the effort if you want to love your life and create a life you love!

A product I love is a hypnosis tool that can literally help you change what you believe about yourself and about life. It is backed by years of brain research and has music filled with frequencies and tones to bring you into a positive state of relaxation. I received a headset when I enrolled for my PhD at Quantum University and the learning programs and stress relief programs made all the difference for me, both as a student and as a person living here today. It is called BrainTap and it will bring you a sense of peace and relaxation you haven't felt since you were a baby.

BrainTap is an excellent relaxation tool to help you sleep well and enter a deep relaxed state daily in order to live your life on purpose and with joy. Using Brain Tap will balance your left and right brain hemispheres and synchronize their function. It also rewrites your subconscious programs to be a positive force in moving away from being contracted by stress and into expanding your life to express all the wonderful gifts and talents within you. Visit my website to click on a link for a free BrainTap trial. You only need a set of headphones or earbuds and a few moments of quiet time to enjoy a wonderful reset for your brain and entire nervous system each day.

My grandmother had a great tool for relaxation before bed; she gave us a glass of milk. The calcium always made us sleep well and wake up refreshed. I don't drink milk before bed anymore, but I do take a calcium supplement. It not only makes me sleepy but helps me sleep relaxed and well. A magnesium bath with Epsom salts and a calcium supplement will put you right to sleep.

Turn off the television and computers at least two hours before you want to sleep. Do not sleep with your phone on your pillow or your laptop in your bed. If you have a lot of trouble sleeping, remove all the electronic devices from your room and see what changes in your sleep. The electromagnetic fields and blue light from screens cause disturbance in the body and stimulate the systems. This causes restless and anxious sleeping in many people. Life is very different when you sleep well versus when you are sleep deprived. I have found sleep to be an essential key to my happiness and mental state. If you are not sleeping well, it is absolutely affecting your reality in a negative way. Be willing to change some things to get good sleep and reality itself will be very different in a positive way!

Many people who struggle with the stress of daily life are supercharged and much more confident and clear on how to solve their problems when they begin to make sleep a priority. If you are stressed and cannot sleep it is only prohibiting you from being rested enough to fix the stressor the next day. Counsel yourself and lovingly put yourself to bed and the world will be brighter in the morning. Be aware that anxious thoughts like to visit at bedtime so be prepared and make bedtime a ritual using the tools we discussed to help you sleep. This will make your life a lot easier. Once your systems are supported by the proper vitamins and minerals and you are claiming rest and sleep as a human right, you are well on your way. The next step we are going to take is....

Chapter Six

The Workout Room

*"We are shaped by our thoughts; we become what
we think. When the mind is pure, joy follows like
a shadow that never leaves."*

– Buddha

Now that we have calmed everything to a healing state, it is time to get intentional with our energy and our power! The world isn't going to stop turning just because you have anxiety, but know that you can handle anything that comes your way today. This is where the magic of the strong new you happens. How is that going to happen?

You have to re-frame how you see stress and your response to it. All stress isn't bad. We must stress muscles to become strong. We must push through to accomplish a goal. The brain is wired to solve problems; it enjoys a challenge and will grow new neural connections when we learn something new. We grow bored if we are not challenged and that can lead to destructive behavior. This idea leads us to the workout room where we get strong and confident, while we stretch and grow.

Viewing stress as a positive if it motivates us towards a goal retrains your system to respond to positive stress in a positive way. Ask yourself when an event occurs, "Is this pressure that can cause me to respond in a positive way?" If so, how can you grow and change to conquer the task at hand? When you think this way, the brain releases dopamine in the pleasure center of your brain as a reward for your growth. This translates into the awesome feeling we all get when we faced it and aced it.

Re-framing your thought pattern for accomplishment/reward, rather than survival/fight or flight sends your thoughts to the frontal cortex rather than the enlarged amygdala. Thoughts now literally move through a different channel in your brain than the old stress response! The more times you feel stressed and have success re-framing it, the more your brain begins to fire in this new pattern until the stress response changes. It now causes you to rise and succeed. Your attitude about stress and its purpose in your life is what determines this new brain pattern. You get to oversee this process by thinking about stress differently.

If you need help moving into this pattern, try doing something you know you can control, like riding a rollercoaster or some other activity that involves a bit of anxiety and reward. It does not have to be a rollercoaster; it can be anything that scares you or challenges you with a guaranteed safe outcome once you face it. Notice the good feeling you have afterward and be with the concept of how your brain works so you can create more conditions to train your brain. Taking back your power and gaining confidence is a major factor in conquering anxiety and loving your life.

Most people under chronic stress feel their life is out of their control. They feel trapped or forced to be in a situation until it is over with no way out or no ability to change it. This may be true for you and it could also be a perception. Most things can be changed by simply changing the way we look at them. It is always our choice to determine how we see things and what they mean to us.

If you feel stuck or trapped in your life and you cannot see the problem in a new way, you have to find a place of power within your daily routine to start from. What do you have control over and what can you change? Maybe organizing your house or your time would be a good starting place. Maybe you can decide to take a ten minute walk after dinner or listen to a new kind of music on your drive to work.

You can make a choice to do something nice for yourself every day and find a way to do that in five minute increments. Everyone has personal power and choices no matter how confined they feel. Finding a way to see those places in your own life will become a thought pattern that will grow into more personal power. You will begin seeing more opportunities and choices that you might not have seen before. Making a list of things you can change is a great way to start opening those thought channels to loosen the chains you feel binding you to stress and anxiety.

Need help starting? You can cut your hair or dye it. You can change the clothing you choose to wear. You can donate some items to charity and make more room in your house. You can rearrange the furniture. Read a book. Watch a funny movie. Learn new recipes. Pick up a hobby. Stop answering the phone. Play sick for a day and have a break... it does not mean you would choose to do any of those things, but knowing that you could is what makes all the difference. You do have choices and knowing that is very empowering.

The point is, any change you make alters your routine and frees you to think differently.

You can also choose to determine what you are learning from the current situations that are driving you batty. Are you learning patience? What about endurance? Maybe you are learning self-control? On a spiritual level maybe you are learning to ask for help or gratitude? If you are a doormat, perhaps the lesson is developing healthy boundaries. You can always decide to ponder what you are learning, and no one can take that away from you. If the lesson is patience and you develop patience, the circumstance will shift when you have mastered patience.

Sometimes the lesson is learning to walk away from what no longer serves us. If you do not want to walk away, set a goal to improve the situation. Then you can put some energy into learning new ways to approach it. That difference in thinking will trigger the reward center pathway and the situation will look different with this new approach. This is all a journey to reformat the energy systems in your body and pull the plug on the panic that is ruining your life.

You get to decide when the torment will end by taking charge through the exercises in this book! I have a secret for you that you already know. Panic is exhausting! Worry drains you. It is easy to think you do not have the energy to change, but it takes less energy to change your perspective than it does to panic and believe you cannot do anything about your anxiety. You can change it and you will change it. It will be a relief to decide that your life will be different and make it so.

Once you have worked this out it is time to use that energy...

Chapter Seven

The Office

*"Successful people maintain a positive focus in life
no matter what is going on around them. They stay
focused on their past successes rather than their
past failures, and on the next action steps they need to
take to get them closer to the fulfillment of
their goals rather than all the other distractions
that life presents to them."*

– Jack Canfield

The workout room and the office are similar rooms with very different focal points. Now that we have looked at the mental strength training exercises, you are going to put them into action in the office. The office is where you conduct the business of your life. What is your business? That is a deep question and can be taken several different ways. If you do not know what your business is, you might be minding the business of others at the expense of your own. If you do not have any business of your own, then it's time to start making some because this is the room where you set goals and achieve them. Having strength of mind is only useful if you have somewhere to practice that strength and see tangible results in the form of a better life and better dreams.

The office is the place where you have vision. If you do not have a vision for your future that is a major problem; it is a place where anxiety can fester. We have to see a future in front of us or we will have no direction to set our sights on! If you do have a vision for your future, this is the place where that vision becomes clear and the direction is set to move forward. Progress is very empowering and healing. Progress will inspire you to higher thoughts and more productivity in other areas. At the end of the day, you will sleep well and feel a sense of purpose.

To make use of your office space, take some time to set a plan and a vision for what you want your life to look like in a year. What habits will you need to adopt to be the person who achieves that goal? What time will you set aside to make this happen? What will you need to learn in order to be successful? Making a vision board is a great way to put the vision and the steps together for the new life you are creating and the person you will become in the process of attaining that goal. It also serves as a powerful image reminder to trigger the right response in feeding the feelings of a positive future and keeping a focus on the next step.

After making your vision board, you will break the vision into smaller steps you can take to make that vision happen over time. Spend at least 10 minutes a day thinking about your vision or doing one thing to help you move closer to your goal. Many times, doing a lot of small things is more powerful than trying to do one big thing. This will also help you remain positive each day as you move toward your best life. Positivity is the medicine that cures anxiety about the future.

Anxiety is a bully when it comes to killing hope for the future. The voice of anxiety can thwart any excitement about the uncertainty of what is to come. By placing your goals, dreams, and visions in the future space of your mind, you reclaim the excitement that something wonderful will happen as a result of your focus and dedication. You are now in charge of the conversation your brain is having about the future. Anxiety can try to speak, but it won't have a lot of room. Whatever comes up, you will handle it and keep moving toward your goals.

Anxiety can also be a friend in disguise, warning you to handle some things or change something for your own good. If anxious feelings come up, ask yourself, "Is there anything I can do to change this situation I am anxious about?" Anxiety can be motivating because it keeps us from being comfortable when we are not operating as our best selves. If you cannot do anything about the situation, you need to let it go. One way to do this is to write it all out on paper and rip up the paper or burn it. Watching the problem become words that can be made into ash is a powerful picture of what you are allowing to happen inside.

There are several options if you know this is a situation you need to face and take action. First you need to pinpoint the issue and identify the problem so a solution can be found. You can prevent an event from occurring by taking the necessary action before the consequence takes place. You can prepare for a situation that is inevitable by looking at your options and choosing the best action in agreement with your best self. You can postpone an event you are unprepared for by communicating with the people who are expecting something from you and arranging something different. Ask for help if you need it. Talk to someone who can help you take action if you feel frozen by fear. Formulating a plan and writing it down will alleviate a lot of the burden you feel and help you move forward beyond anxiety.

Now that you've got your work done, it's time to play!!!

Chapter Eight

The Game Room

"When you see a child play, and it is so close to seeing an artist paint, for in play a child says things without uttering a word. You can see how he solves his problems. You can also see what's wrong. Young children, especially have enormous creativity, and what's in them rises to the surface in free play."

– Erik Erikson

Play is an important part of life. Whether it is a board game, chess, or throwing a football, play serves a purpose in our lives that moves us into creative problem-solving and higher brain function. If there is no play in your life, anxiety is sure to take its toll on you. We were not meant to work and stress and drag ourselves through life every day without enjoying the happiness of time spent with friends and family in a child-like state of fun.

Making time for play needs to become as important as any of the other things you need for a healthy life. If you have not been making time for play, ask yourself why.

What makes you happy? Getting in touch with what would constitute play for you is the first step. Making that happen is the natural by-product of owning your life and changing the structure from a house of anxiety to the house of your best life. To fully inhabit the house of you, structure your time in a balanced way to take back your power and lead yourself to a new way to live.

Pick an afternoon or evening on your calendar and plan something fun once a week. It can be simple or complex. It can be with a friend or with a group. It can be extravagant or free. Just plan the time once a week and stick to it. Getting away from life's routine periodically allows us to return fresh and full of positive energy. Play allows us to embrace the unexpected and grow to love the surprises in our life without having to control everything. Play gets us in touch with ourselves and those around us. It builds trust.

Certain types of play such as cards, chess and strategic ball games build skills that apply to daily life. Thinking a step ahead, playing your hand and going where the ball will be so you can receive it are all critical thinking skills applied during the stress of competition. These games condition you to enjoy using these skills under pressure. While it is considered playtime, it is also productive. Yet one more way play serves our life!

Tactile play such as art, pottery and sewing are also very calming and rewarding. Making jewellery, photography and cake decorating are also some fun ways to express yourself and bring play into your life. If you don't know where to start, make a list of things you enjoy and things you enjoyed as a kid and look into free events near you that match those things on your list. It won't be long before you have a lot of wonderful things to look forward to each week!

Take some time now to make play a priority and plan some playtime activities that will create memories. Make space in your house, your life and your calendar for joy and happiness. Nothing chases away anxiety like laughter and knowing you have friends and family always nearby to face life events and succeed in whatever comes your way. These happy memories also serve you in times of sadness that may come. Fill your memory bank with great stories and moments that will be with you for the rest of your life.

On the flip side, too much play can also cause anxiety through knowing you are not being responsible. If this is the case for you, know that play is much more rewarding when it comes after taking care of the business of life. Play is not really any fun when there is an unresolved task hanging around nagging at you, needing to get done. Being honest with yourself is liberating. The truth shall set you free and that includes freedom from anxiety. Look at the level of play in your life and keep a balance between work and play. Both are important.

In the game room is a cabinet with a little play village. There are tables and chairs and little people who can walk down imaginary paths to visit the houses in this play set. We all had little people play sets as kids and setting up worlds for the little people to live in is something every child enjoys. This is one of the first games all humans play because from a very young age we are finding out how we fit into the world around us and studying relationships and what that connection means.

I know a man who lives in Uganda in a Village called Kyela. The people are very poor and there are over 200 orphans. Looking at the pictures, I noticed how happy the people and children are. He asked me about my village. I tried to explain that we don't have villages in America. We call them communities.

The people of Kyela Village have worries, but not anxiety like we do. There is a sense of 'us' that brings the village together to help solve problems for the good of the whole village. There is also a connection between the people that they are doing life together; they share joys and sorrows as a group.

Looking at Kyela, I have given a lot of thought to how important community is in everyone's life. If you do not have a sense of community, there is a vulnerability inside that feels very sad and anxious. With that in mind, I will give you some suggestions for building a community or joining one to satisfy this basic human need in your life. Everyone needs a tribe.

You can volunteer somewhere that provides a service to a cause that is near to your heart.

Join a book club or special interest club that is formed by a group of people enjoying an activity together.

Attend a church or spiritual service in your area. Keep attending new groups until you find one that reflects what you believe and feels like a match to your inner self.

Form your own group and make time for important people in your life. Don't be too busy to keep the connection with important people. Relationships with people you enjoy are really what makes life so special. These are also the people who encourage you and pull you out of despair when you're having a tough time. Time is the cement that holds it all together, so make time and create good memories with your tribe.

Take a deep breath and move to where things grow and breathe...

Chapter Nine

The Garden

*"When the world wearies and society fails to satisfy,
there is always the garden."*

– Minnie Aumonier

Now, we are going to step outside to the garden. We will sit by the reflection pool and dip our toe in the water... watching the ripples move toward the water's edge. After all the work you've done, let's take a deeper look into what makes you peaceful or anxious and gain some wisdom on how to move forward on every level. Being in harmony with yourself is the ultimate key to living a healthy, happy life.

The garden is where we plant and grow. It is where we reflect and dig deep into ourselves as we see the soil and the water and the web of life. The garden holds the fruit of what we have tended and the weeds that are choking our prized roses. One issue that can cause our harvest to be weak is when the two fields within us aren't harmonizing.

What are the two fields inside us? The heart field and the mind field. Both have been studied and measured. While we think they operate independently, they work best when there is coherence between them that links to our breath. This state of unity brings a deep peace regardless of what is happening around us.

Some anxiety comes when we are not in alignment between our heart and our mind. If there is a battle between your heart and mind, the two fields that are supposed to work in harmony are at odds and the struggle is intense. The heart field is much stronger than the mind field. These are measurable energy fields and the strength difference is important to be aware of because when a battle ensues, the mind will tire itself trying to be right. Allow peace between the two and leave room for a solution to emerge. Just be with it and decide what your peace is worth. If nothing else, it is not worth your peace to struggle over something endlessly.

Learning to trust your heart is a very important part of life. This is why healing the past trauma is so important. Without healing of trauma and ceasing to blame, you can never trust your heart. If your heart is the strongest energy field and you wrestle with mistrust of yourself, then the mind has to work overtime. If you have anxiety over a decision, it could be that the heart and mind are in battle. At that point you need to make peace with yourself first and get in touch with the argument between the heart and mind before you can really move forward.

Find a space and time to be with yourself about it; pray about it or talk it over with someone whose wisdom and integrity you trust. Meditate on it and release it; ask for a right feeling to come upon you so you know what to do. The truth is many times we do know the right thing to do. We just do not want to do it because we are afraid or prideful or whatever other feeling is trying to hold us back when some part of ourselves really wants to grow. If you spend some quiet time and go within, the answers are always inside you. It may take time, but they are there. Sit quietly and place your hand on your heart. Feel the rhythm as you breathe in and exhale out this drumbeat that is the song of life. Feel yourself get centered. Deep inside is the answer and in the stillness, you will have a deep knowing and the integrity to follow your truth.

Trust the process. It is a journey worth taking and the reward is getting your life back in a form that you love. From that point on it is yours. You are no longer who you were. Yet, you are not who you are going to become either. There is a certainty and consistency to you that will remain throughout your life. If honesty is important to you, then you will remain so until the very end – no matter what anyone else does. That certainty is stable and comforting.

Give yourself time to contemplate the deeper meanings of life without rushing or compromise.

Practicing self-care is very important to reclaiming your place in life and repurposing your energy. Stop running away from the anxiety; turn around and embrace taking steps to handle anything coming your way. Self-care is an act of kindness toward yourself. It means you matter. It is developing a new relationship with yourself. To develop that relationship, you must spend time with yourself. The more you do this, the less other people will be able to define you. You will know who you are, and that confidence will flow through to your present and future plans. Spending time in self-care and self-reflection is also very supportive in creating boundaries between you and the rest of the world. The more you enjoy your inner peace and happiness, the less you will be willing to sacrifice those things to make other people happy. Maintaining healthy boundaries will not be a negative or stressful event. It will come naturally as you honor yourself without taking anything away from those around you.

The last place we are visiting is the property line. Walk the edge of your life. Survey the landscape that is you and see the fence between your life and the rest of the world. Be aware this is yours and you can do whatever works for you in this place. As you grow in understanding yourself and your journey, the line between you and not you will become clearer. In time, everything that happens will not feel like it is happening to you, it will be happening for your growth. You will handle whatever comes your way. You will create a state of peace and joy and stability and be more selective in what you allow into your mind and heart and life.

At the same time, you are also open to change and new ideas. Opportunities will come along that add spice and flavor to your life, that is something we all need. While we crave predictability, we also need some unpredictability in our lives to generate new ideas and thoughts. That keeps a healthy amount of new life in our brains and spirits. This life is an adventure and we all need to be the hero in our own story sometimes. Keep that in mind as you evict the ghost of anxiety within you. See stressful situations as being there to serve you so you can show up and conquer them! It is hard to be an overcomer if there is not anything to overcome. Without a little obstacle or problem to solve there really is not a story. Nobody wants to watch a movie where nothing really happened.

Make this the chapter of your life where you discover yourself and get healed! Life starts now! This is the beginning of a whole new time for you. Embrace your sensitivity and carry with you all the wisdom and compassion you have gained in this journey into healing.

Gaze once more past your boundary, there is something there...

Chapter Ten

The Sanctuary

Beyond the property line is the horizon where sky meets land. It leads us to gaze upward to the heavens and within ourselves at the same time. The sanctuary is as far as you can see and also inside your spirit. This is the place where you are sacred and all of life is sacred and a beautiful mystery is waiting to be revealed.

Throughout history, humans have sought a spiritual connection to support them in their journey through life. Whether they need guidance, forgiveness, wisdom or protection, religion and spirituality span the history books in many forms from the earliest recorded civilizations.

Having a purpose and a belief in something greater than yourself is a valuable strength that many people explore and develop. It builds a faith that we are not in this alone and some force greater than us cares and is there to help us. It is a perspective that says there is no failure, only growth in who we are in every moment. It's the belief that life is more than just what we see with our eyes.

Faith and anxiety cannot occupy the same territory. Finding a greater power – whatever that means for you – and beginning to surrender those problems that are too heavy for you to bear, is a comfort that many people experience. Build your sanctuary of peace by connecting to that greater power in whatever way works for you.

If you do not know what you believe, spend some time asking yourself the bigger questions; what would it look like and how it would feel to cultivate faith that the weight of the world is not on your shoulders every day? Contemplate grace and mercy and love and blessings. Look at the stars! Look at the beauty in nature and sunsets and the song of the birds. All of creation is singing a song and you are a part of that song too!

Knowing there is a bigger purpose to life helps put today's stress in perspective and prepares your heart for good things to come. I believe you were created for a purpose and that purpose is good. Do not be afraid to ask for help. Do not be afraid to be honest. Do not be afraid of the awesome person you will become when you master your house and live in it fully!

Keep in mind how many people you are going to share this information with and help because of the discovery you have made. You are a creature unlike any other! I am glad you took this tour with me and I invite you to share your story and your experience on the online book club at: www.HealWithHolly.com

About the Author

Holly Hudspeth was born in Nashville, Tennessee. She graduated from Belmont University with a major in Broadcast Communications and a minor in Journalism. She has a Master's in Quantum Natural Medicine from Quantum University, is an Institute for Integrative Nutrition certified Health Coach, and is trained in Neuro-linguistic Programming (NLP).

Holly recovered from stage 4 Lyme disease and mold exposure. This illness allowed her to explore alternative medicine at a deeply personal level and gave her a deep compassion for other people's healing. Holly enjoys travel and currently resides in St. Augustine, Florida.

If you are serious about living the life of your dreams and evicting your anxiety **join the online community and Welcome Home Program** that will include:

- A PDF journal

- A weekly video series covering the topic of each chapter in greater detail

- A weekly group coaching call

- A closed group Facebook page so you can connect with others on your journey

- Options for private one on one coaching with Holly herself for extreme transformation

For pricing and to sign up now please visit
www.HealWithHolly.com